The Day I Met Myself

Selected Poems by Peter Gammond

ISBN 978-1-78281-984-4

Cover photo by Jane Bown CBE
Publishers Jules Gammond & Edward Adams

CONTENTS

THE DAY I MET MYSELF

I turned a sudden corner
and, like an angle-mirrored mime,
mad and miraculous,
walked into myself.
I put it boldly
for that is how it was . . . .

He (that is me)
was just as I'd expected;
apparently off to see about a death
still publicly unsuspected;
spickly out of fashion
with just enough awry
to baffle the careless critical gaze
of a passing eye;
three new books just bought
and ill-afforded;
eyes full of magazines and music
and face carefully worded,
with the hair in a hurry
through the mist of a cigarette;
and I've no time to talk of money . . . .
at least . . . . not yet . . . .

It was a summer morning
full of cats and coal-trucks,
taking its failure with a casual air.
Bad luck, good luck
scattered like waste-paper;
and the street a long tongue
panting in the quivering heat;
and quite a number of songs unsung
doomed to be incomplete

He walked through the streets
as I would walk through a cornfield;
he stared boldly at people
as I might stare at an oak-tree;

5

he was as smart with answers
as I was at snubbing thrushes;
he was as innocent of guile
as I was newly-born;
he was a walking wakefulness
of all I wished to be.
In this amorous mood of magic
I was gratified to meet me.

The pavement threw up hot kisses.
Sweetly my thoughts and a bus collided.
Soft were the shocks of my smiles
On those who derided.
The beautiful women of fiction
and the old men in sad stories
walked through my dream
in a rollick of tram-rides and lorries.
'Love you', I cried, 'I will not
for love I've thrown out of my word-list!'
Some threw back 'like' or 'admire'
and not many missed.

I turned,
wanting to watch my passing back,
and caught a sidelong wink
and a whispered laugh of a word –
'Man . . . what do you think . . . think?'
I turned, to catch up,
Wise with the wishes I saw.
And I walked by myself
to myself
in meticulous awe!

From *Poetry from Oxford* edited by Dennis Williamson. Fortune Press, 1950.

AT ST. ENODOC

Beneath a flowing Cornish sky
in Enodoc's snug arms I lie
at rest below the trampled grass
where Pentax-bearing trippers pass
and, as this simple stone they see,
say 'Betjeman? Now who was he?
or, 'Betjeman! Now he did well
with all that verse he used to sell!'
Though one or two have come to pay
Their kind respects and gravely say
'God rest his dormied soul in Heaven;
he scored a decent seventy-seven!'

In peace I lie and sweetly dream
of searching in that boggy stream
for Penfolds hooked from lofty tee.
'Is yours a four?' 'No, mine's a three'.
Then, prodding in the lovely muck,
A brand-new ball is found. What luck!

I lie now nearer to the green
Than with most shots I'd ever been.
And, on a dry and running day,
showers of golf-balls come my way,
descending not from source divine
but from an ill-struck number nine,
while, echoing down to Daymer's shore,
I hear the distant cry of 'Fore!'

I slumber in these hallowed grounds
Contented to be 'out of bounds'.

From the film *Betjeman's Britain*, 1990

THREE LOVE POEMS

1. OF A DAY PAST

Long on a lovelorn afternoon
we lay in the heat and the haze of this hill,
and the grass and the slip-sky tell me now
if I loved you then I must love you still.

The rough patch boys on the stones below
undressed and dived in the handspan pool,
and the lazy lust of our belly bed
said I was a thief and you were a fool,

for I stole the light of your brown wide eyes,
and I copied the feel of your firm bare arm;
you gave the song of your love away
and neither one there saw the deed do harm.

Long, my light love, have the years gone by
and fever and falsehood have had their fill,
yet the memoried touch of your thigh still says
if I loved you then I must love you still.

From *Oxford Poetry 1950* edited by J.B.Donne & Donald Watt

2. THINGS THAT WERE RIGHT ALL THREE

As I went wondering down the street
on a wayward, skyward day,
I met a girl with dancing feet
and a sun brown face
and shining lips and lucky hair
and a yes-blue hat,
and her clothes all neat and clean.
She might have been out of some Greek fable;
she might have been Venus or Helen – or Grable . . .
or Jane or Jean.

And on the right was a house I'd seen,
red-ribbed, roofward growing;
with a bright brass nose and arms of green
on to a garden holding;
and its eyebrows rough and its roses red;
and its eyes were clear and flashed like a banderilla.
It might have been built for a new St.Paul's
or a house for a lord with a dozen halls . . .
or a suburban villa.

The street was cluttered with chattering tongues
and a babel of silent thoughts.
Sin from the branches boldly hung
as I passed the boards
of the cemetery fence; the gas-lamps lit;
and the orange peel
(smell of kippers) and coal-cart load.
It might have been down the Appian Way.
On the Rialto or the Rue de la Paix . . .
or the Banbury Road.

The girl was as good as a Turkish bath
to sweat the slumber from me,
and the house was as fine as a stage design
road-led to me.
Oh, apple-right logic, clean wave pattern
and sweet tooth touch,
with song made out of a splinter.

The girl, the house, and the road - all three –
were made and loved and lived for me;
Spring day, Summer way, Autumn come
and all the Winter.

From *Oxford Poetry 1950* edited by J.B.Donne & Donald Watt

3. A CHRISTMAS VALENTINE

The love that I shall send you now,
this most inconstant of all days,
is not, I rather sadly say,
(but say it truly all the same)
the kissing and the gaming type
we played with when young love was ripe.
The love that I shall send you now
is fifty years and more in age.
It does not ramp. It does not rage.
It lies upon life's printed page
And cannot be erased.

The love that I shall send you now,
This most commercial of all days,
cannot be said in lightweight verse
and silly pictures – even worse.
It must be said in long known looks,
in deep-worn pages of old books,
in Schubert trios, Mozart songs.
Maybe it can't be said at all,
living where all true love belongs –
wrapped up in sighs.

14 February 2011.

AUTUMN ELEGY

Out we walked into a deep-noted autumn evening
Brooding on false verdicts; for truth
turned stone, wood and leaf into meaning
and tore down starred sky for a frail roof.

The night stirred slowly into a thousand proverbs
each more pointed as our wonder grew;
arms linked, mind stroking gently on the words
that fell fungoid on our grass-green mood.

Till on a sudden level lay the lake below.
The deep translucence of black negatives,
in a simile of mirror, sky and burnished gold,
pummeled its silence on our naked ribs.

Fearful in the emptiness of love we stood,
and the dark daring of our frightened thoughts;
we threw circling reasons into the black pool,
hoping our outward boldness seemed a sword.

Heart of us frail on the darkening water,
mind of us lost in time's false romance;
sad for us the sense of a god's blind murder,
and our own dumb birth so carelessly planned.

From *Oxford Poetry 1949* edited by Kingsley Amis & James Michie

A CHRONICLE OF THE MONTHS
(with appropriate opening and closing music)

JANUARY
(Music: Prokofiev: Classical Symphony – slow movement)

What shall survive us?
What shall survive?
What, in this cold start, will touch
the waiting heart of earth as urgent,
to bring love out again so surely,
making us wonder why and hourly
that human loves are not resurgent;
while this clod earth, most dead alive,
stores love warmly and so much?
Bare-boned limbs of trees do mock us,
fingering the sudden clouds,
ripe with rooks in raucous crowds.
We don't control the winds that rock us
but mystery is on our side.
We shall survive you!
We shall survive!

FEBRUARY
(Music: Enesco: *Rumanian Rhapsody* – opening)

Old bones wake cold
to the stars' gaze.
New bones dance
around the grave.
Old bones shiver
at death's look.
New bones bristle
full of blood.
Old bones know
this year's their last.
New bones with love
are singing mad.

MARCH
(Music: Shostakovich: *Moscow Cherumusko* – dance)

First to breath the new-born air,
the poet cuts a sonnet out;
pours a kettle of despair;
drinks it like a March wind's shout.
Now he slaps a limerick
fresh as paint against his wall;
now a rondelle on the quick,
old man's agony to gall.
Limbered up and full of metre,
eyes alight and ideas neater.
Ready to record it all
in his usual free-verse sprawl.

APRIL
(Music: Sardana – introduction)

Walled in a womb of earth
the warm seed stirs,
catching the curious eye
of a hungry bird;
thrusting a whitened hand
above the earth;
meeting a sudden death
as quick as birth.
Warm in the thrush's throat
it sighs content
and does not know
its lifelong spell is spent!

MAY
(Music: Elgar: 'The Spanish Lady' – overture)

May – when the dancers angle
light on the bridge of sighs;
when the maidens set a-dangle
the young men's eyes.
May – when such sweet unease
has stirred their song;
when the weak are bled by tears
and only the tears are strong.

JUNE
(Music: Spanish jazz)

Poppy red is the throbbing heart of the street
aflame with summer dreams
and the ragged wounds of the sun.
Pin hot pains pinch the searching feet
of a man alive only in his guesses,
dead to all but everyone.
While a love he has not
(or a love he has)
cottons on to his brain and leaves it reeling,
unable to feel in the sharp ache of feeling.

JULY
(Music: Josef Strauss: *Die Libelle* – polka schnell)

The bloated world
lies fat in profitable ease,
no longer living on its capital
but lush in the rich takings
of a greenback growth.
A world we should dislike,
less eager-eyed to please:
that gold-toothed smile
is not gold hard at all
as plump brown hands
draw in a season's rakings.
To like we may be loathe:
but plain joy strikes
the proper note
that makes us like this lore
that scatters riches
on the idle poor.
And thus we lie
and watch with surfeit joy
while life-long breakers
kiss the coloured shore;
thinking only ever,
promising only more.

AUGUST
(Music: Beethoven: *King Stephen* – female chorus)

Melon-ripe to bursting
sulks the heart,
torn twixt a virgin tease
and a willing tart.
Sulks that the virgin
waits for the winter drought;
sulks that the tart
will see but summer out.

SEPTEMBER
(Music: Mozart: Symphony No.29 – slow movement)

Brown and reluctant
moves the summer's thigh
closer to winter's clasp.
Breast full of harvest
ripe for an old longing.
Head full of sea-spray verse
For a chill month's singing.
Nipples alert at the cold touch.
Eyes rather troubled
that reaping takes so much.

OCTOBER
(Music: Sardana – introduction)

The alert and darting eye of the robin
glints with an old man's glee,
full of a stolen life
from the dying tree.
While other loves have lost
the war of hours,
he stores a private lust
drawn from the withered flowers,
and, piping weirdly
songs of bright defiance,
mocks the spendthrift day
with his and God's alliance.

NOVEMBER
(Music: Grieg: Symphonic Dance (Beecham))

Cramps assail us,
the sheets are damp,
the cold fog of doubt almost hides
the light of the lamp.
So this was the prize –
the splutter of coughs and the groans:
deeply adrift and too late
the knowledge of being alone,
The Summer is past and, not on your life,
is Winter a one to worry you into a wife!

DECEMBER
(Music: Prokofiev: 'Classical' Symphony – slow movement)

So, what has survived us?
What has survived?
Except the mice that have nested,
the bees that have hived?
We shall give you a present
this Christmas, this season of grace;
a brand new and smug for your gazing
immaculate face:
sharp with the lesson
of one now so nearly alive . . .
that we, of all season and sea-change,
that we have survived!

VERSES BETWEEN NOW AND THEN

THE INGENIOUS CHILD

Mine was a childhood full of thoughtless reasons,
a sort of epic lunacy with logic in control,
full of north-country quakery and quackery.
Half my life was Sunday and half my life was Saturday.
The rest was just a blank time;
A for-what-we-have-we-thank time;
and I was a brown-skinned, leggy lad
as awkward as a foal.

The starched and Sunday collar was an ineffective flattery
Designed to send my halo winging like a lark . . .
I preferred some scanty bathing trunks beside a muddy river
with no thought of wherefore and no thought of whither.
Was content to be a smart boy
while my really heart-to-heart boy
went grubby and un-noticed
through nature's jungled park.

Grand-parents so respectable, created with their clothes on;
the vicar's hand so heavy to subdue the inward revel.
My parents watched me growing, an interest-paying treasure,
for the banks or civil service surely made to measure.
Not a precocious from-the-south boy
But a butter-in-the-mouth boy.
I contrived to climb mountains
while I walked on the level.

I really was a horrid little devil!

WHEN WE WERE YOUNG

When we were young the days were long
and every hour was time for song,
and every minute seemed an hour
and every modest weed a flower.

And every day a special task –
What it was no need to ask;
And every day a ritual dish . . .
Friday, of course, reserved for fish.

Saturday for playing games
and gossiping and dropping names.
Sunday for church and choking tie
and leg of lamb and apple pie.

And every day was full of trust;
the heart aflame with golden lust!

FOR ANNA AND A DAY

Summer sun; Winter snow;
Autumn brown and Spring aglow.
These are days that, through the years
We've shared.

Winding cliffs, yellow sands,
Devon lanes and foreign lands . . .
We have wandered hand in hand
And cared.

No need to worry now
about our penny thoughts:
no secret can a promised heart
withhold!

Tell me where and tell me when.
Say you love me now and then
as I, content in loving you,
grow old.

POEM WRITTEN JUST NOW

Hey down, honey down,
Someone bring the money down.
Then no further fret or frown –
For plenty of honey
And lots of money
Is as good as a golden crown.

I took out my wallet
And looked inside
At my private wealth.
Not a lot to hide.
After tedious counting
I glumly found
Just a hundred and thirty
Thousand pound.
Which may seem rich
For the labouring poor,
But not very much
For a man like me
Who ain't gonna work no more,
No more,
Who ain't gonna work no more.

Hey down, honey down,
Someone bring the money down,
And then no further
Fret or frown.
For plenty of honey's
As good as a golden crown.

From *The Pale Blue Book of Nonsense Songs* unpublished 2015

ODDMENTS

THE SAD STORY OF A NOBLE CHILD
WHO DIED EXCEEDINGLY YOUNG

The Hon. James Augustus Enderby-South
Was born with a silver spoon in his mouth.
Sadly, he'd scarcely taken a breath
When he swallowed the spoon and was choked to death!

SOME MUSICAL LIMERICKS, in Bb,Op.336

A young Court Composer from Linz
Wrote and complained to the Prinz
That for writing his stuff
He was not paid enuff.
And nobody's heard of him sinz!

A charming young lady called Anna
Attempted to play the pianna.
While performing some Liszt
Quite a few notes were miszd.
But they said that she had a nice manna.

VERSES WRTTEN BETWEEN NOW AND THEN

1. SONG OF A SUN-WORSHIPPER

Rays of sun have rounded edges,
soft to touch, to love, embracing
bird song bright beyond comparing
dolling up the dance-wide street;
making wherefore into therefore
by its certain easy sharing,
smile enticing, love complete.

Artficial light has corners,
pointed anguish to our seeing,
cutting ruthless wounds in darkness –
ghastly gas-lamp grinnng wide;
electric answer – not a chance, sir,
to avoid the avid starkness
of its braying homicide.

I have watched the candled miser
bent to eye wound in its goldness,
watched the neon painted faces
worn to superficial oldness.
Give me one light, loving sunlight,
trickbox of a thousand graces;
liquid gladness, plump and full!

THE DAY I SNUBBED MYSELF

In a street where old rebellion died away
and each stray glance adagio with ease,
only the wind was in boisterous mood
stirring the dust and the threadbare trees.
The bookseller's sign was a sign from God
that nothings in knowledge was strange or odd.
A blasé cat and a ballet-struck leaf
went aloof in their classical grief,
one un-mated, the other divorced
by a stagestruck sycamore, bankruptcy-coursed.
An elegant day on its futile way
ignored my feet in the settling dirt
nor cared for my principles – nor my shirt –
when, who in the tide of time should I meet,
dressed in reflection down the street,
than myself again, my brother's keeper,
a version of Verlaine – but slicker and cheaper.

I'd like to have hid from his hello face
but the genial square gave nowhere to hide
as he minced along, a smug machine
turning all rubbish to tight-skinned pride.
You'd have thought it was Wren with a brand-new plan
instead of a one-book writing man.
He turned for a greeting that garrulous day
but I looked ineffably other way
like a photograph of Japan,
as coyly as Eve when the game began;
for its often wise to avert one's eyes
from shadows as sland'rous as silhouettes
and all other selves that self begets.
Such things are better left unseen.
So I played him dirty and cut him clean.
Yes, damn the man, I cut him dead,
and may the Devil share his bed.

www.ingramcontent.com/pod-product-compliance
Lightning Source LLC
Chambersburg PA
CBHW071803020426
42331CB00008B/2390